CONCERTO
FOR
CLARINET

BY
ARTIE SHAW

FOR SOLO Bb CLARINET WITH PIANO ACCOMPANIMENT

Music Sales America

DISTRIBUTED BY

HAL•LEONARD®
CORPORATION

7777 W. BLUEMOUND RD. P.O. BOX 13819 MILWAUKEE, WI 53213

Concerto For Clarinet

Piano

Artie Shaw

* From here to letter G figures are written for 4 Sax's and also 4 Clarinets.
  Use either section but not both.

SOLO Bb CLARINET

CONCERTO
FOR
CLARINET

BY
ARTIE SHAW

FOR SOLO Bb CLARINET WITH PIANO ACCOMPANIMENT

Music Sales America

DISTRIBUTED BY

HAL•LEONARD®
CORPORATION
7777 W. BLUEMOUND RD. P.O. BOX 13819 MILWAUKEE, WI 53213

Concerto For Clarinet

B Flat Clarinet

Artie Shaw